Table Of Contents

Notes To Students

Using This Book

This review text presents an overall view of the history of the United States people. It is a study of the beginnings of the United States government under the Constitution and a survey of United States history from 1865 to the present. Careful use of this review text will help the student prepare for a Competency Test in U.S. History and Government.

Throughout the course, students are asked to look at 13 constitutional issues. A chart listing the 13 issues can be found just before the Glossary and Index. Throughout the book we have printed a special symbol (shown at left) to signal you that one of the 13 issues is being discussed. At review time, it will help to go through the book, look for the symbol, and re-read the marked paragraphs.

Thirteen Enduring Issues

1. National Power - limits and potentials
2. Federalism - the balance between nation and state
3. The Judiciary - interpreter of the Constitution or shaper of policy
4. Civil Liberties - balance between government and the individual
5. Rights of the Accused and Protection of the Community
6. Equality - its definition as a Constitutional value
7. The Rights of Women under the Constitution
8. Rights of Ethnic and Racial Groups under the Constitution
9. Presidential Power in Wartime and Foreign Affairs
10. Separation of Powers and the Capacity to Govern
11. Avenues of Representation
12. Property Rights and Economic Policy
13. Constitutional Change and Flexibility

Since these issues are the core of the course, you should center your attention on them. An appendix at the end of the book has suggested procedures for a year-end review, and we have again listed examples of the *"Thirteen Enduring Constitutional Issues."*

Basically, there are two ways to use this book:

1. An All-Year Drill Book

The preferred way is to work with it all year long, either in class or at home to check your knowledge of what you're doing in class and what you've been assigned to read in your textbook. Try to fill in the questions gradually and check your work with your teacher. The filled-in material then becomes a good summary for you to read and study at the end of the year.

N & N

United States History
and
Government
A Competency Review Text

Authors:

Paul Stich
Wappingers Central Schools
Wappingers Falls, New York

Susan F. Pingel
Skaneateles Central Schools
Skaneateles, New York

John Farrell
New York Archdiocesan Schools
Cardinal Spellman High School, Bronx, NY

Editors:

Wayne Garnsey and **Paul Stich**
Wappingers Central Schools

Cover Design, Illustrations, and Artwork:

Eugene B. Fairbanks
Granville, New York

N & N Publishing Company, Inc.

18 Montgomery Street   Middletown, New York 10940
1 – 800 – NN 4 TEXT

Dedicated to our students, with the sincere hope that

United States History and Government - A Competency Review Text

**will give them an appreciation and understanding
of the historical events and people that have shaped our country.**

Special Credits

Thanks to the many teachers that have contributed their knowledge, skills, and years of experience to the making of our review text.

To these educators, our sincere thanks
for their assistance in the preparation of this manuscript:

Cindy Fairbanks
Kenneth Garnsey
Anne McCabe
Walter (Skip) Mendle
Virginia Page
Victor Salamone

Special thanks to our understanding families

United States History and Government - A Competency Review Text has been produced on a Macintosh Quadra 840AV and Apple LaserWriter Pro 630.

MacWrite II and *MacDraw II* by Claris and *Canvas* by Deneba Software were used to produce text, graphics, and illustrations. Original line drawings were reproduced on a Microtek MSF-300ZS scanner and modified with *Photoshop* by Adobe. Formatting, special designs, graphic incorporation, and page layout were accomplished with *Ready Set Go!* by Manhattan Graphics.

Special technical assistance was provided by Frank Valenza and Len Genesee of *Computer Productions Unlimited*, Newburgh, New York.

To all, thank you for your excellent software, hardware, and technical support.

© Copyright 1988, 1998
N & N Publishing Company, Inc.

Printed in the United States of America

SAN # 216 - 4221   ISBN # 0-935487-20-4

6 7 8 9 0 Bookmart Press 2000 1999 1998

Unit One

Constitutional Foundations

For The United States Democratic Republic

1700	1750	1790

•Albany Plan •Declaration of   •U.S. Constitution
                    Independence   •Bill of Rights

• Enlightment

•Locke •Montesquieu •Rousseau   •Articles of Confederation